How to Subtly Tell Your Partner You Want More Sex

David Adams

ISBN: 9798478701000

DEDICATION

I would like to dedicate this book to all the partners out there with a sense of humor.

CONTENTS

ACKNOWLEDGMENTS

I would like to start by thanking my wife for putting up with my ridiculous ideas and humor.

CHAPTER 1
WHY ARE YOU HERE?

First off you may be wondering, why is the font so big? Why are the sentences spaced so big? Why are there even words inside the book? These are great questions, but I am not going to answer any of these questions until later in the book, and maybe not even then. The book just started, relax.

You are probably here because your partner doesn't

want to have sex as much as you do. This is the case in 50% of relationships, which is a statistic I completely made up by talking to two different people I randomly saw walking down the street. One told me "go away I don't want to talk to you" and the other said "my wife is sleeping with my brother, so yea I guess."

I am going to tell you that together we are going to get through this, but honestly you are going to physically do it without me, I'm just a book.

I need some time to think of helpful stuff that sounds deep and important, so take your time getting to the next chapter. So, enjoy some pictures.

```
    *o..*
_*_o....O.*
____0.*..o.O......o.......*
_O...o......0*..o*:......*
_$$$$$$$$$$$:..o0:::.O*
_$_________$::*:.....o:....0
_$_________$..o:O*:.0:...*.
_$_________$_$$$$$$$$$$$
_$111111111$_$_________$
_$111111111$_$_________$
_$111111111$_$_________$
__$1111111$__$111111111$
___$11111$___$111111111$
____$111$____$111111111$
_____$$$______$1111111$
______$________$11111$
______$_________$111$
______$__________$$$
______$___________$
______$___________$
______$___________$
_____$$$__________ $
__$$$$$$$$$_______$
___________________$
_________________$$$
_______________$$$$$$$$$
```

____________________¶¶¶¶¶¶¶¶

___________________¶¶

__________________¶¶

_________________¶¶

________________¶¶

_______________¶¶

_____$$$$$$$$$$$$$$$$$$

_____$_______________$

______$________ZZZZ$

_______$_____ZZZZZ$

________$__ZZZZZZ$

_________$ZZZZZZ$

__________$ZZZZ$

___________ZZ

____________$$

___________ $$$

__________$$$$$$

________$$$$$$$$$$

______$$$$$$$$$$$$$$

CHAPTER 2
POEMS FOR YOUR TROUBLES

Hot and Heavy

You went to bed all hot and heavy,

Ready to burst just like a levy,

But you were shut down just like a computer,

So you broke down, feeling neutered,

They've got a headache, or not in the mood,

So, you go to the living room and make some comfort food.

Birthday Sex

Tonight's the night for birthday sex,

It has been a while, So I search for the latex,

There it is! I found it hiding,

Between the nightstand and some siding,

I grab the wrapper practically gliding,

Smiling ear to ear getting ready for the riding,

But that's when I see,

They are asleep they have forgotten me,

Oh well, my birthday will come next year,

So, I shed a tear, and crack a beer.

Flowing Locks

I got my hair cut, I hope they notice,

But they are watchinga speech from POTUS,

I walk in the room with my flowing locks,

But their eyes are locked on the TV box,

I clear my throat trying to catch a glance,

But my efforts are useless, so I lose my pants,

This also doesn't work, am I even here?

Or am I in a different dimensional atmosphere.

CHAPTER 3
HAVE THEY SEEN IT YET?

Alright at this point, I want you to just enjoy reading this book while laying in bed next to your partner. Hold the book at such an angle so that it would be borderline impossible that they don't see the cover in all its glory.

CHAPTER 4
HOW ABOUT TRY A DIFFERENT SPOT

SERIOUSLY? STILL? Okay if they didn't notice you holding the book in bed all night, I got some serious questions for you. Did you hit on their brother or sister? Did you forget their birthday? An anniversary perhaps? These drastic times call for drastic measures.

You need to leave the book in a place that they MUST see it. Here is a list of my top places for you to leave the book.

#1. On the toilet seat (make sure the toilet seat is down with the lid closed. I don't want to hear "directions unclear I put my book in the toilet water.")

#2. On the driver's seat of their car.

#3. Brew them a cup of coffee and put the book on top of the coffee cup or make them a nice dinner and set the book on top of the plate.

#4. Put the book on their pillow.

#5. Tape the book to the door handle of your front door so they can't leave without seeing it.

CHAPTER 5
YOU ARE STILL HERE?

I don't have anything good to say for chapter 5. You might as well just skip to the next chapter.

CHAPTER 6
TRY SOMETHING NEW

I mean, is sex even that important? Okay, okay, it is, it is. I am running out of ideas here, what have you tried so far? What was that? Your upset because now I am asking YOU for advice? I guess that's fair. Have you tried literally just talking to them about it? Ha! I know, that would be insane to have an adult conversation like that. Can you even imagine how vulnerable you would be? Opening up like that? Have you tried texting them? Have you tried being super passive aggressive until they ask you what's wrong and you say "nothing." Damn, the passive aggressive angle usually works so well.

CHAPTER 7
HMM THAT DIDN'T WORK?

So, if leaving the book in places they would see it, being super passive aggressive, and texting them didn't work…hmm…lets see if the next chapter has any useful information for a change.

CHAPTER 8
HEAVY SIGH

I still got nothing. Oh! How about I just give you some advice I have learned over the years to help cope with my dry spells of intimacy.

Tip #1: NEVER, I MEAN NEVER, start cooking with dirty dishes in you sink or a dirty workstation. Seriously, clean that mess up before you tackle dinner. If your dishes are already clean, hell yeah good job.

Now you're ready to fill up your sink up with some soapy water and wash the dishes you are using to cook WHILE you are cooking. I can see it now "directions unclear I washed my food." DON'T do that, wait until you are done cooking the food and wash it AFTER your done with the pan/pot.

Tip #2: If you have trouble remembering to brush your teeth and floss, do it in the shower. My floss game has gone up 1000% since I started flossing in the shower. Everything is better in the shower. Have you ever tried having a beer in the shower? Treat yo self.

Tip #3: Put a roll of garbage bags at the bottom of your garbage can. But wont it get gross under there and all wet? NO! and if it does, why the hell is your garbage can that gross? Take it out more often, sicko.

Tip #4: Buying a croc pot or an insta-pot can make anyone look like a good cook. Also, buy a rice cooker. I must be hungry, most of these tips are food related. I'm going to grab a snack. *Several minutes pass* Okay, I'm back.

Tip #5: Brew your own coffee, unless you don't want to, then don't.

Tip #6: If you have literally been doing nothing all day while your partner is out working hard all day, at least look productive when they first walk in the door.

Example: You have been binge watching The Office on Netflix for the 100th time, and you have watched several seasons in one day. Uh oh, your still in your pajamas and your partner is coming home. DO SOME DISHES or get dinner ready. Maybe even brush your teeth and put on some clothes if you're feeling extra motivated. Don't have your first impression be a bad one.

CHAPTER 9
ARE YOU SURE YOU HAVE A PARTNER?

I think it's time to ask the hard-hitting question of are you even in a relationship and/or do you even have a partner?! Once you have figured that out you will be ready for chapter 10.

CHAPTER 10

THE BOOKS NOT CUTTING IT

Sorry to let you down. I feel like we have grown so close to each other during this whole experience. Maybe you feel the same? Maybe put some of that energy you put into getting so close to me, into time with your partner. Good luck my friend, this is the way.

ABOUT THE AUTHOR

I can't believe you are even still here. Honestly, I am flattered. I don't have anything exciting to write about myself, so I won't waste your time…unless you want me to. Okay if that's what you want, then here it goes. I am a dad, with a dad bod that I have accepted isn't going anywhere anytime soon. I decided to grow out a mustache for no shave November. It doesn't look very good, but it brings me joy, so I got that going for me.

2021-2022 CALENDAR

Here is a calendar to keep track of all the days you are successful in the bedroom!

Place an X for each day you are not successful and put √ each day you succeed. I recommend using a red ink for X and green ink for √.

EXCUSE LIST 2021

Use this list to write down each excuse you are given for why your partner doesn't want you in the bedroom. I filled in some of the most popular responses.

#	Description	Tally Marks
1	Too Tired	
2	I have a headache	
3	Didn't we have sex last month?	
4		
5		
6		
7		
8		
9		
10		

January 2021						
Sun	Mon	Tue	Wed	Thu	Fri	Sat
					1	2
3	4	5	6	7	8	9
10	11	12	13	14	15	16
17	18	19	20	21	22	23
24	25	26	27	28	29	30
31						

February 2021

Sun	Mon	Tue	Wed	Thu	Fri	Sat
	1	2	3	4	5	6
7	8	9	10	11	12	13
14	15	16	17	18	19	20
21	22	23	24	25	26	27
28						

March 2021						
Sun	Mon	Tue	Wed	Thu	Fri	Sat
	1	2	3	4	5	6
7	8	9	10	11	12	13
14	15	16	17	18	19	20
21	22	23	24	25	26	27
28	29	30	31			

April 2021

Sun	Mon	Tue	Wed	Thu	Fri	Sat
				1	2	3
4	5	6	7	8	9	10
11	12	13	14	15	16	17
18	19	20	21	22	23	24
25	26	27	28	29	30	

May 2021						
Sun	Mon	Tue	Wed	Thu	Fri	Sat
						1
2	3	4	5	6	7	8
9	10	11	12	13	14	15
16	17	18	19	20	21	22
23	24	25	26	27	28	29
30	31					

June 2021						
Sun	Mon	Tue	Wed	Thu	Fri	Sat
		1	2	3	4	5
6	7	8	9	10	11	12
13	14	15	16	17	18	19
20	21	22	23	24	25	26
27	28	29	30			

July 2021						
Sun	Mon	Tue	Wed	Thu	Fri	Sat
				1	2	3
4	5	6	7	8	9	10
11	12	13	14	15	16	17
18	19	20	21	22	23	24
25	26	27	28	29	30	31

August 2021						
Sun	Mon	Tue	Wed	Thu	Fri	Sat
1	2	3	4	5	6	7
8	9	10	11	12	13	14
15	16	17	18	19	20	21
22	23	24	25	26	27	28
29	30	31				

September 2021						
Sun	Mon	Tue	Wed	Thu	Fri	Sat
			1	2	3	4
5	6	7	8	9	10	11
12	13	14	15	16	17	18
19	20	21	22	23	24	25
26	27	28	29	30		

October 2021						
Sun	Mon	Tue	Wed	Thu	Fri	Sat
					1	2
3	4	5	6	7	8	9
10	11	12	13	14	15	16
17	18	19	20	21	22	23
24	25	26	27	28	29	30
31						

November 2021						
Sun	Mon	Tue	Wed	Thu	Fri	Sat
	1	2	3	4	5	6
7	8	9	10	11	12	13
14	15	16	17	18	19	20
21	22	23	24	25	26	27
28	29	30				

December 2021

Sun	Mon	Tue	Wed	Thu	Fri	Sat
			1	2	3	4
5	6	7	8	9	10	11
12	13	14	15	16	17	18
19	20	21	22	23	24	25
26	27	28	29	30	31	

EXCUSE LIST 2022

Use this list to write down each excuse you are given for why your partner doesn't want you in the bedroom. I filled in some of the most popular responses.

#	Description	Tally Marks
1	Too Tired	
2	I have a headache	
3	Didn't we have sex last month?	
4		
5		
6		
7		
8		
9		
10		
11		

January 2022						
Sun	Mon	Tue	Wed	Thu	Fri	Sat
						1
2	3	4	5	6	7	8
9	10	11	12	13	14	15
16	17	18	19	20	21	22
23	24	25	26	27	28	29
30	31					

February 2022						
Sun	Mon	Tue	Wed	Thu	Fri	Sat
		1	2	3	4	5
6	7	8	9	10	11	12
13	14	15	16	17	18	19
20	21	22	23	24	25	26
27	28					

March 2022						
Sun	Mon	Tue	Wed	Thu	Fri	Sat
		1	2	3	4	5
6	7	8	9	10	11	12
13	14	15	16	17	18	19
20	21	22	23	24	25	26
27	28	29	30	31		

April 2022						
Sun	Mon	Tue	Wed	Thu	Fri	Sat
					1	2
3	4	5	6	7	8	9
10	11	12	13	14	15	16
17	18	19	20	21	22	23
24	25	26	27	28	29	30

May 2022						
Sun	Mon	Tue	Wed	Thu	Fri	Sat
1	2	3	4	5	6	7
8	9	10	11	12	13	14
15	16	17	18	19	20	21
22	23	24	25	26	27	28
29	30	31				

June 2022						
Sun	Mon	Tue	Wed	Thu	Fri	Sat
			1	2	3	4
5	6	7	8	9	10	11
12	13	14	15	16	17	18
19	20	21	22	23	24	25
26	27	28	29	30		

July 2022						
Sun	Mon	Tue	Wed	Thu	Fri	Sat
					1	2
3	4	5	6	7	8	9
10	11	12	13	14	15	16
17	18	19	20	21	22	23
24	25	26	27	28	29	30
31						

August 2022						
Sun	Mon	Tue	Wed	Thu	Fri	Sat
	1	2	3	4	5	6
7	8	9	10	11	12	13
14	15	16	17	18	19	20
21	22	23	24	25	26	27
28	29	30	31			

September 2022

Sun	Mon	Tue	Wed	Thu	Fri	Sat
				1	2	3
4	5	6	7	8	9	10
11	12	13	14	15	16	17
18	19	20	21	22	23	24
25	26	27	28	29	30	

October 2022						
Sun	Mon	Tue	Wed	Thu	Fri	Sat
						1
2	3	4	5	6	7	8
9	10	11	12	13	14	15
16	17	18	19	20	21	22
23	24	25	26	27	28	29
30	31					

November 2022						
Sun	Mon	Tue	Wed	Thu	Fri	Sat
		1	2	3	4	5
6	7	8	9	10	11	12
13	14	15	16	17	18	19
20	21	22	23	24	25	26
27	28	29	30			

December 2022						
Sun	Mon	Tue	Wed	Thu	Fri	Sat
				1	2	3
4	5	6	7	8	9	10
11	12	13	14	15	16	17
18	19	20	21	22	23	24
25	26	27	28	29	30	31

YOUR LOVE LIFE JOURNAL

Printed in Great Britain
by Amazon

34941616R10053